This Guide to Life has
been presented to:

EGMONT
We bring stories to life

First published 2009 by Egmont UK Limited
239 Kensington High Street, London W8 6SA

Copyright © 2009 Hanna-Barbera
™ & © Hanna-Barbera

 ™ & © Warner Bros. Entertainment Inc.
(s09)

Text by Carolyn Madden.
Design by Cali Hughes and Faye Dennehy.

ISBN 978 1 4052 4859 4

1 3 5 7 9 10 8 6 4 2

Printed in Singapore

Please note: this book contains risqué humour. It is ideal
for the young at heart, but not suitable for children.

The Hanna-Barbera
GUIDE TO LIFE

Cool Tips for Top Cats!

EGMONT

CONTENTS

Hey, hey, hey, folks!

Like – er, me and my cartoon cronies were drawing lots as to who should open the book, and guess who got the short straw?

Matter o' fact, they were all the same length – I fixed it 'cos I wanted to get my name up front, in the stars! I wanna be big, big, BIG!

So if the burden of life is weighing heavily on your shoulders, step right this way and allow ol' TC and his pals to guide you through those mysterious sticky patches with a few stories and pearls of wisdom. Dip in, dip out. I can guaran-darn-tee you won't come out the same on the other side: your pockets will be lighter, at least. Only joking there, pal, only joking!

Welcome, cool cats, to the wacky cartoon world of Hanna-Barbera.

Most sincerely yours,

Top Cat

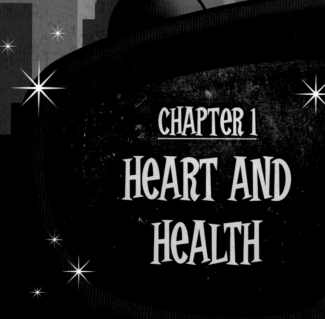

CHAPTER 1
HEART AND HEALTH

THE FLINTSTONES' GUIDE TO LOVE

The Colm N. Tater Interviews

Hey there! It's your roving reporter, Colm N. Tater, here, with our very own stone-age lovebirds (or should I say love-pterasaurs?), Fred and Wilma.

CT: Can you share with us the secrets of a happy marriage after all these years?

W: Well, it's not been that long! But, yes, I'd say we're lucky to have each other.

F: Too right, Wilma's my rock. Who else would get my mastodon pelt this clean?

CT: Fred, some women might see you as a little unreconstructed. Do you help much around the house?

W: Does he? Well, sorry to interrupt,  but if leaving his rock collection lying around counts, then he's a gem.

F: Whaddaya mean? I bring you flowers, don't I?

W: Fre-ed! It was a cactus from the service station, but it's the thought that counts.

F: And I make your day happy and bright, don't I, Wilma . . . honey?

W: Yes, dear. Just the sound of your voice yelling, "Wilmaaaa!" sparks my flint. And, of course, you're *never* grumpy.

F: Well, just occasionally I'll read something in the *Daily Slate* that gives me cause for concern. Or maybe Barney puts a rock in the works . . .

W: Hee, hee, hee, then I say to my friend Betty, "Uh-oh, I hear the call of the male Gripe-o-saurus!"

F: (*Blushing*) Oh, shucks.

CT: And now to family life. You've got little Pebbles, of course. Any more chips off the old block planned?

W: Goodness me, no.

F: I haven't drunk home-brewed cactus juice since . . .

W: Pebbles is perfect, thank heavens for little girls, but she's got Bam Bam to play with so we don't think she needs a brother or sister.

F: Pebbles keeps us busy day and night. Ow! Keeps Wilma busy.

CT: Well thank you, Mr and Mrs Flintstone. Any last marital hints for our readers?

W: R-E-S-P-E-C-T.

F: Eh? What's that, Wilma?

Top Ten Marital No-nos
by Fred Flintstone

These marital top tips have all been tried and tested . . .
and landed me in the dino dung quicker than you
can say 'tyrannosaurus rex'.

1. Don't clip your toenails in bed: those flints spark enough to start a fire!

2. Never talk with your mouth full of bronto-burger: the spray can be lethal.

3. Sunday lunch? Don't chew the bones.

4. Don't forget to use your biggest club when picking her some roses so she knows how much you love her.

5. Taking the lady out clubbing? Don't wear the pelt your mother gave you last birthday. There ain't nothin' sexy about the scent of damp mastodon!

6. When weeding the rock garden, always wear your longest pelt so that Betty next door doesn't get a shock. Those gals talk, you know.

7. Offer to take the woolly mammoth to the wash – even when it's not your turn.

8. Don't complain when she whips up a batch of rock cakes. You can always get granite dentures next time you visit the dentist.

9. Don't forget to remove the tick-picking pterosaur off your hair before you enter the bedcave.

10. Leftover stegosaurus stew is not to be used to glue the wheel back on to the rockmobile. At least, not while she's watching . . .

And remember folks, whatever you do,

Yabba-dabba-doo!

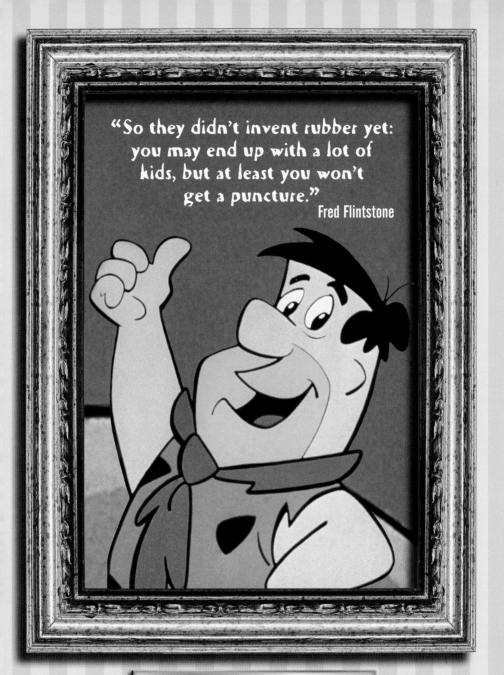

"So they didn't invent rubber yet: you may end up with a lot of kids, but at least you won't get a puncture."

Fred Flintstone

· A Little Moment of Calm ·

17

Captain Caveman's
Guide to Eternal Youth

Captain Caaaave-maaa-aa-aaan!
Unga bunga. Me caveman, you need help.
Me never get old.
You say, "Uh?"
Me say, "Unga zowie, here's how-ie."
Tee, hee, hee.

Cavey keep all mod-cons in pelt. Me find can-opener or torch when Cavey need it. No problem.

Me got big hair. Wrinkles hiding.

Dee Dee comb Cavey's back hair each day.

Me love Teen Angels. Me like 'em all. When me sees 'em, me see pink hearts. Love make Cavey young.

Captain **Caaaave-maaa-aa-aaan** like shouting. Keep lungs clear. People can hear shouts. No need repeat. Repeat make anger. Shouting means no anger.

Me dye hair with henna. Cavey's mummy recipe. Hide grey.

Cavey keep fit. Shout. Fly. Bash. More fly. Catch baddies. Unga bunga.

Me no perfect. Me have problem getting flying power some days. Cavey's club go all weak. Me eat powdered brassica. Make Cavey parp. Help Cavey fly.

Me sleep in prehistoric glacial ice block. Mmm, comfy. Make skin cool and soft – ahh.

Me got good teeth. Me chew bones. Taffy get Cavey 'electric toothbrush'. That creature small but brave. Me eat it. Unga. Good teeth.

Cavey only look 1, 2, 3, 4 . . . um, 700,000 years old. Unga-zowie!

YOGI and FOOD

A Friend's Guide to
Obsessive-compulsive Greed

by Boo Boo Bear

Er, well, hallo there, reader. Boo Boo here. Oh boy, oh boy! Does Yogi have a problem with food. Now I don't wanna sneak on him or nothin' but I fink he gotta stop. I tells him, "Yogi, the Ranger won't like it if there's an overweight bear in the Park." But he just says, "Don't worry, Boo Boo. This is one bear that bears himself well, even when he's bare."

When Yogi's sniffin' after a pic-a-nic basket, I tells him that animals eat to live, only humans get hung up about food and he doesn't want to become a human, does he?

So Yogi replies, "What's the problem with being human, they never stop eatin'. Boy, oh boy, oh boy!"

I can't really win, can I?

MATTERS OF THE HEART
WITH DICK DASTARDLY
The Colm N. Tater Interviews

Hankies at the ready, your very own sheikh of shorthand, Colm N. Tater, caught up with *Wacky Races'* own handbrake heart-throb, Dick Dastardly, to ask his advice on matters of the heart.

CT: Dick, have you ever been in love – and was it reciprocated?

DD: There was one who stole my heart. Dolores was her name. It was back in my circus days: I was the 'Tyrant of the Trapeze' and she 'Dolores and the Dancing Dogs'. I would soar, she would sashay. I would fly, she would foxtrot. I would ... well, you get the picture.

CT: 'Love in the Ring', it all sounds very romantic. So, what happened?

DD: One day a new act arrived. 'Leopold the Lion Tamer'. He was a jumped-up jackass. Lion Tamer my foot, he had a bag of kitty treats and a big whip! Leopold pranced into the ring with his phoney accent and magnificent head of hair, and swept my Dolores off her feet. I watched it all from my perch on high. It was their kiss that caused my downfall. My terrible accident. My moustache's … I can't go on!

CT: There, there, Dick. So … there's never been another?

DD: No, no. Many a dame has glanced my way and then glanced away – I cut a dash with the ladies you know – but I'm true to my first love.

CT: Do you have any advice to readers who may be having trouble finding love?

DD: Yes. First, consider your image. Turn to Dashing Dick for fashion advice, my look always gets the girls giggling. Finally, if you see someone you like the look of, stride boldly up to her, seize her hand and ask her to marry you. Women love decisiveness. If I'd wooed my Dolores into wedlock swiftly, instead of twirling around the Big Top, her head wouldn't have been turned by that leonine lump. There'd be a Mrs Dolores Dastardly by my side and even a little Dickie or Dolly. Ah me, there's nothing left but regrets.

Ahem, well, that's all folks! Mr Dastardly left the interview muttering something about cracking the whip and poisoning the friskies. Ha, ha. Bye for now!

HONG KONG PHOOEY's
Guide to
Personal Training

The Lamb Chop

(position 1)

(position 2)

The Stinking Doufu

The Striking Walrus

Let me hear-ya-say, "Hoo!"
Let me hear-ya-say, "Ha!"
Let me hear-ya-say, "Hoo-ha!"

Dat's it. Now all ya need to do is throw a few shapes and ya got 'em bad guys slinking back in to the shadows. Whassat? Keep fit? Oh. Cool. Yeah. So, you wanna like do some stretches and then throw the shapes? Watch me, the King of Kong-Phoo.

The Mee Krop Krup

Arthritic Adder Pose

The Furious Warthog

The Pat-a-cake

PARENTING TIPS
FROM FRED FLINTSTONE

Parents! Colm N. Tater here. Don't let the kids get the better of you. Here's our very own Fred Flintstone with, shall we say, an old-fashioned approach to child-rearing. Very old-fashioned. In fact, it's positively stone-aged. Over to you, Fred ...

DISCIPLINE

See, er, don't say so to Barney, but he lets that Bam Bam run wild! I'm a firm believer in a bit of discipline: a quick rap over the knuckles with a solid bone spoon when they've been chewing the

mammoth skin rug soon sorts them out. I've never had to do that with my Pebbles 'cos that little sweetie's just as cute as a toggle. She's daddy's little

T-rex. She only has to wrinkle her nose at me – and bash me on the head with a shin-bone – and I see stars.

ROUTINE

All kids benefit from a good routine. Pebbles has a regular day cut out for her. Y'know, she gets up, she eats some gruel with honey, she

gets dressed in her softest pygmy shrew pelts, then er, well, Wilma does the rest. But I tells her, "Wilma, the child needs routine. And what my cute-a-saurus needs, my cute-a-saurus gets." I'm a family-oriented kinda guy.

FUN AND PLAY

Well, kids nowadays, they got it all, see. In my day, we had sticks. That's it. Just

sticks. We bashed things with 'em, hit each other, poked dead dinosaurs, rubbed 'em together 'til yellow hot stuff came ... boy, did we get in trouble for that! Kids today, they want bones, big bones, little bones, bones with holes in, bones made into necklaces, they even want them in their bedcaves, I ask ya. And skins, you know that Bam Bam, he's got one stretched tight over this hollow log, right, and he bashes it with sticks. Makes a crazy kinda sound, 'BAM-BAM-BAM!' Guess that's where his name comes from. It'll never catch on though. Ain't no toy for a boy.

SLEEPING

My little Pebbles is just like her da'. Cuddle her up in her old bearskin and she's asleep in ... er ... real quick! It's all about feeling safe, see. We've got Dino standing guard outside, ain't nothin' gonna get past that brute. So, my darlin' honeybee's gonna sleep safe and sound.

HEALTHY EATING

You can't expect a baby to get its gums around a Stego-steak, they need mushed roots and shoots, berries by the bundle and a little minced pterosaur breast. Hee, hee, I did try Pebbles on a Brontoburger last week. Ya know, the little cub just spat it out, 'Pah!' Just like her ma. I gotta say, parenting rocks!

Teen Angst and Me
by Judy Jetson

You old folks think you got it tough! Try being a teen in 2062. Well, Judy Jetson's a match for anything, and I'm here to tell you how to de-program the key irritations of teen life.

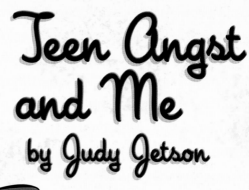

Parents

Much as I love them, Mom and Dad are really uncool. They don't listen, they say stupid stuff and they don't let me do anything. At least when you're an oldie – 'adult' I think you say (joke!) – you can do what you want. No one tells you when to go to bed or school, you can go swimming anywhere in the world with no Mom to tut at your mini Instant Stretch™ bathing costume ('Just add water and watch the boys fizz!'). Tee, hee! The only way to handle elderly folk is to adjust the truth a little. Say I want to go swimming in Mexico – half an hour by jetbus – I tell the olds I'm stopping off at the Primitive Science Museum to look (laugh!) at the automobiles people used to drive along the ground. I tell Dad that Mom said it was OK and Mom that Dad said it was OK. As long as they've said OK to something you've asked them that day, then it isn't really a lie.

Siblings

Elroy is cute but annoying. All he thinks about is hover-basketball and anti-gravity boots. I can't get near the 3-D TV for sport! The only way to handle him is with good, old-fashioned blackmail (something to do with over-ordering from the auto-fridge) and if that fails, bribery. That kid just loves Starfizz™ candy.

Dating

Well, I haven't really started dating as such, at least that's what I tell Mom. But there are so many cute guys and so little time, I can never make up my mind which one I like best. My friend Mimi got herself cloned so she could try out the football team . . . but then all the clones just argued over who was the best so she had to have them vaporised. Decisions, decisions. At least when you're old and married you're stuck with one person so you can't really change your mind too often.

Exams

School's OK. I love Sports and Ancient History – we're looking at the mid-twentieth century when they had these quaint things called 'Hippies' who did 'Flower Power'. It all sounds so 'way out'! I must ask Mom if she remembers it . . . But exams are the pits. Ever since the 'Cheat' program emerged, everyone has had to stop using computers and had to learn to write with a pen on paper like in the olden days. I mean, how primitive! They'll be expecting us to do math in our heads next!

First Jobs

I've got a part-time job at Inter-Galactic Travel, but I'm just answering the videophone. The pay's bad, only 500 bucks an hour, but I may get a trip in the teleporter next week. That would be so way out!

Conclusion

So, you see, oldies, life's no picnic on the moon for teens either. The difference is, we don't moan about it. End of lesson.

Judy x

Surviving Family Holidays
by the Jetsons

Hello, folks! Welcome to the future. We caught up with those space-hopping robo-heads, the Jetsons, to get some advice on surviving prolonged exposure to the family. Here's George, Jane, Judy and Elroy to tell you how . . .

GEORGE: Hi people, thinking of taking the wife and kids to the moon for a spot of shade? Or stuck at your skyhome over the long winter break? If the thought fills you with fear, you're not alone.

JANE: George! How could you talk like that? Our little family capsule is just perfect, thank you . . . And anyway, what with planning, shopping, cooking and cleaning, it's me that should moan.

JUDY: But Mom, you just press a button and it's all done!

JANE: Well, let me tell you, I've got 'push-button finger' from all that pressing.

GEORGE: As I was saying, there are ways around the trials of family bickering – I mean – life. I recommend the beaches of Outer Zoiker, the women there have one more asset than most!

JANE: George!

GEORGE: Well, Jane, distraction is one way to keep yourself sane under familial stress. What would you suggest?

JANE: What about a nice family game?

ELROY: But Mom, last time we played Twist-It™, Judy said I was cheating for fitting myself with Robo-limbs™.

JUDY: You were! The rules say, "No prosthetics or anti-gravitational devices may be used by human players." Oh, I see your point, the rules stress 'human' not dork.

ELROY: MOM! Tell her.

GEORGE: Kids, we're missing the point. These folks want to know how to survive stressful family situations, not watch one unfold! Now, any ideas?

ELROY: Separate houses?

JANE: Elroy! Now, a family that eats together stays together . . . so what about picnics?

GEORGE: In winter? Well, I suppose you could take a self-heating basket or hire a loco-sun to create an ambient spot for you mid ice-flow.

JUDY: I think other people are the key. Let's have a party and invite the football team. They can talk sport you know, Dad, Elroy.

JANE: Maybe Judy has a point. We could invite the Gammarays from SkyPod 39 and nice Miss Quark from Zogon Avenue. I'll make some star-punch and mooncakes; I think Rosie the Robot can handle the rest of the food.

GEORGE: Great. Other people.

ELROY: Do I have to come? I'm not brushing my hair.

JUDY: What'll I wear? Mom, I need something new. Let's shop!

And with that, this reporter left the Jetsons to their arguing, er, I mean, party planning.

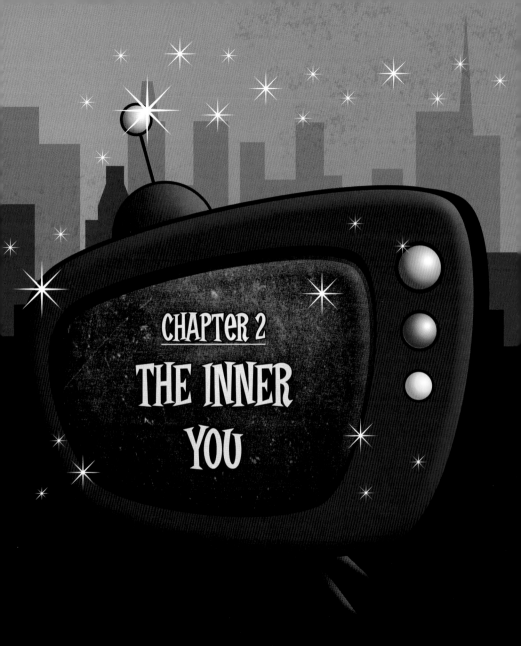

CHAPTER 2

THE INNER
YOU

NURTURING YOUR SELF-ESTEEM

The Colm N. Tater Interviews

You wanted a superhero, we got you one. Space Ghost may be able to fly and even teleport. He's defeated more baddies than you can shake a rattlesnake at. And yet, not even he can dodge the dumps from time to time. Yes, his career has taken such a slide, that he's now a talk-show host!

CT: Space Ghost, welcome to the opposite side of the microphone. How does it feel to sell out in front of a camera?

SG: Don't worry, everyone, I've yet to be delivered into the Claws of Doom. I've still got my powerbands!

CT: But you're washed up. Your enemies are retired, dead or working for you. What does a superhero do if there's no one to fight?

SG: They are? But Moltar, surely he's still cooking up a storm in space?

CT: Moltar was captured by you and subsequently employed as producer of your talk show.

SG: Oh yes . . . I remember now. Zorak then. Surely his mandibles are macerating some innocent alien somewhere?

CT: No, nothing quite as gruesome as that. He spends his time making appearances on cheaply produced television spin-offs.

SG: No! Aw man, that's bad. Mettalus?

CT: He's gone nuts. There's no one left, Space Ghost. How do you keep your self-esteem intact when your very raison d'être has gone?

SG: Where there's a tight, white bodysuit there's a way. That's my

motto. Now I don't fight bad guys, I fight boredom. There'll always be a need for light entertainment so I've switched seats and I'm giving the world what it needs: chat – on my network programme, *Spaaace Ghooooost: Coast to Coast.*

CT: And you don't feel emasculated at all? You don't feel it was all a waste of time?

SG: There's a lesson here, somewhere. A superhero never gives up, even when his mummy says it's bedtime. No. Never. NEEE-VARR!

CT: Thanks, Space Ghost. We'll, er, remember your advice.

Dastardly's Guide to Anger Management

Me? Angry? My dear reader . . . you'd be ANGRY if you were thwarted every step of the way by the stupidity of a team of goofs and a smelly, sniggering mutt. *(Calm down, Dickie Boy, watch the old ticker. Breathe. Ahh.)*

So, how do I cope so well? Let me tell you. Underneath my calm, slick appearance, I'm RAGING inside. You may see a beatific smile on my face but my teeth are gritted and my fingers are knotted with the effort of controlling myself. Surprised, friend? Well, my acting skills are legendary: remember I have more than one televised series to my name.

However, enough about my prowess. You've come to me on bended knee to beg help controlling your temper. Here's how, knucklebrain. The invoice is in the post. *(Chortle.)*

Physical Containment

Feel your blood pressure rising? You'd be amazed how long you can keep the lid on, as it were, if you fix your face into a grimace, teeth bared, and make claws with your hands. Then if the lid does blow, it's an easy transition to slip out a snarl and rip a tissue into teeny-tiny-tiddly pieces with your own BARE hands! Believe me, this is often all that is required to get that lid back on top of that tumult within.

Kick the Dog

Not really, reader, goodness me. You'll have those animal rights people on to me again. Don't be so silly, nothing so unsophisticated as physical abuse. No, no, no. (Have my lawyers approved this?) You can achieve the same palliative effect by:

1. Taking back medals . . . or treats if you don't have medals. The look of disappointment on that whiskery face is sooo soothing.

2. Sending them on an even more impossible mission, so that when they fail – and fail they will – you can shout even louder. Most cathartic.

3. Flinging yourself to the ground, weeping. They'll be so taken aback, they won't know what to do. And of course, a real man is not afraid to cry with frustration. Think about that easy shot you goofed. Go on, chump, let it out.

Feel the Need for Speed

Do I have to spell it out, numbskull? Just get in the car or plane and floor it. (Try to remember to take the handbrake off first.)

Drat, drat and double drat!

Shout it Out!

Find yourself a suitable catchphrase and let rip whenever times get tough: the plan crashes, burns and makes your cloak smell of smoke; the Gen-er-al phones you just as the pigeon slips away; your flies won't do up – then suddenly they do. All these things try our patience. They do, reader, they do. So when this happens, fling back your head, stamp your foot and howl: "Drat, drat and double drat!"™

Please note: this catchphrase is protected by law and may only be used upon receipt of a licence, obtainable from: RM Dastardly, Dastardly Towers, 13 High Street, Dastardlyville, Republic of Dicaragua. A scale of payment is applicable, dependent on the number of 'Drats' used.

STRESS-BUSTERS!

We all need a little guidance to help us over life's speed bumps. We've gathered together pearls of wisdom from your favourite Hanna-Barbera characters. Let's find out how they deal with the curveballs life throws at them . . .

When things get a little rocky, I head for the golf course with my old pal, Barney Rubble. Get myself a hole-in-one and a cactus juice at the clubhouse and I'm feelin' fine. Of course, yelling my personal mantra at the top of my voice, ideally when Barney's just about to take a swing, really helps to capture that feel-good vibe: "Yabba-dabba-dooooo!"

Cavey no get blue. Me go for a nice cut 'n' blow. Yeh, yeh, yeh, yeh, yeh! Look sweet, feel sweet. Dat Cavey.

HANNA-BARBERA'S
TOP TEN
STRESS-BUSTING TIPS

10 Talk about it. But not too much, OK?

9 Keep active. Ahh-eee-ooh-atcha!

8 Get a hobby. Nose-picking is not a hobby.

Well, well, well. TC here isn't one to let life a-get on top of him, see. If things start to smell a bit fishy, I just put on my eyemask, plug in those old earplugs and snuggle me down for a lil' ol' catnap in my trash can. Ahh, life couldn't be sweeter!

As the Master of Connivance, I rarely allow life to get the better of me. I simply dream up a plan more wicked than the last and change my situation by sheer strength of character. Just occasionally, I vent a little frustration in the form of "Drat, drat and double drat!" I've found this so much more cathartic than pulling wings off flies.

7 Eat well. A pic-a-nic a day keeps the doctor away. Two gives ya stomach ache.

6 Drink well. Like-er, don't dribble.

5 Hand your 'to-do' list to your boss. After all, they're so much better than you.

4 Write it down. Then no one else has to listen to it (see 10).

Well, you know folks, if I feel a little crushed, I just talk to my old friend, Dum Dum. He doesn't usually have anything useful to offer, but at least I can be grateful that I'm not that stupid.

Well, according to the history books, stress was a 20th-century phenomenon and was banned in 2019 by the Global Union's first President. Since, then, yours truly just takes himself to the Auto-Rub for a quick massage or the Auto-ECT for a brain reboot (it's only 5,000 bucks and you'd be amazed at how it numbs the pain).

3 Do good. Get out there and help someone less fortunate so that you get to feel superior.

2 Listen to music. Get some cool toons to smooch to and get those she-lines over to P-A-R-T-Y. Oww!

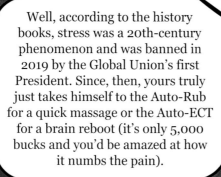

1 Each night, write down three good things that happened that day. Neighbour's car got clamped? Write it down.

60 SECOND INTERVIEW THUNDARR THE BARBARIAN

Greetings! Colm N. Tater here to interview the man that put the 'der ...' in thunder, Thundarr the Barbarian!

TB: So Tater, why did you summon Thundarr? What do you want of me?

CT: Er, welcome, Thundarr, er, Mr Barbarian, er, sir. Can I ask you a few questions?

TB: I have the Black Pearl in my loincloth. I cannot fail to answer you truthfully.

CT: Quite so. Er, so you're a barbarian, eh? How's that going?

TB: By the Sunsword of San Fran, I have the power to seek out injustice and quash it, as my enemies seek to quash me. What's not to like?

CT: You have a trusty team in Princess Ariel and Oolak the Mok. Could you handle the baddies without them?

TB: You doubt the strength of Thundarr? I, who can leap unlikely distances from metal birds to the top of ruined 20th-century skyline icons and defeat an army of groundlings with a swipe of my Sunsword. I, who can gallop for twenty days on my white stallion and throw priceless treasures at the Statue of Liberty. I, who can even resist looking at Princess Arial in anything other than a fraternal way. I need nobody! But it's quite nice to have a chat with the Mok from time to time, since he can't answer back.

CT: You lead a primitive lifestyle despite having the ruined trappings of the Technological Age around you. Don't you feel you're missing out not utilising all the mod-cons of the 20th century?

TB: Who is this 'Mod-con'? Does he dare to challenge Thundarr the Barbarian? Let him raise his sword against me! I will defeat him and defend my right to wear an animal pelt and moon boots. I am Thundarr the Barbarian!

CT: Absolutely. Yes, you are. Well, thanks, Thundarr. We'll leave it there.

Secret Squirrel Investigates:
Paranoid Tendencies

Pssst. Yeah, you. Shh! My name's Secret Squirrel and here's my assistant, Morocco Mole. He's a mole. From Morocco. This much you've deduced, eh? Not bad for an amateur. You need a secret agent, eh? I'm your rodent.

So, you think someone's after you, eh? You feel eyes upon you in crowded places? Things happen that you can't explain? Strangers look at you in a knowing way, eh? Eh? There are four possible explanations:

1. **you look odd;**
2. **you have memory loss;**
3. **someone is after you;**
4. **you are paranoid.**

Let's examine the evidence, eh?

1. If strangers are staring, maybe there's something about you that attracts their attention. Are you fabulously good-looking? No. Are you famous? No. Are you wearing just your underclothes? No. That brings us to one of two conclusions: either you're paranoid or they're after you.

2. Let us consider point two. Either you have memory loss and it is actually a family member staring at you . . . or they are after you. Or you're paranoid.

3. Now for point three: someone is after you. Why? What have you done? Are they CIA? FBI? MI5? TW1TS? Are they henchmen? Will it hurt? STOP! No one's after you. You're just paranoid, see point four.

4. OK, here's the deal. As a professional, I must advise that you take the 'Are You Paranoid? Quiz' to find out how paranoid you are. Adios, amigos! And remember, don't look back, eh?

Are You Paranoid? Quiz

Q1: *You're lying awake in a strange bed and get the heebie-geebies that someone's watching you. Do you:*

A: turn over and tell yourself not to be silly;

B: move rooms;

C: put the light on and check the room, then sleep;

D: upturn all the furniture and check behind the spooky portrait on the wall for spyholes?

Q2: *You're walking down the street and almost step on a manhole with the cover missing. Do you:*

A: assume it's a silly mistake and carry on;

B: sue the council;

C: take a bit more care walking along;

D: don't turn around but check in every reflective surface you pass to see who's following you?

Q3: *Your passport draws some interest at the customs desk. Do you:*

A: wait patiently. You did look a bit odd with blue hair;

B: clear your throat loudly and ask what the problem is;

C: step up and try to charm the customs officer into thinking you are normal;

D: make a run for it? Only twenty yards to freedom!

Answers

Mostly As:
you're one cool cookie. Whoever's got you in their sights better show themselves now.

Mostly Bs:
upfront and decisive, there's no messing with you. Let's hope your nerve holds when they've got you in the cellar.

Mostly Cs:
you know they're out there, but as long as they stay out there, that's fine.

Mostly Ds:
yup, you're paranoid.

Dastardly's Guide to (Repeated) Failure

Me again, dear reader. I imagine that I've been invited to give you the benefit of my wisdom not because I fail but because I overcome failure. D'you see?

How best to guide you, dear reader? Via a bank, probably (heh-heh-heh, a little joke to start play).

There's one recurring theme here: when, despite my best efforts, misfortune befalls, I pick myself up, dust myself down and start again, like a moth, bashing into the lampshade, plink, plink, plink! But inside I'm growing, reader, I'm learning. I'm thinking, *Try, try, try again, Dickie, old boy.*

Let's take some scenarios as examples to study, shall we?

Picture the scene. As I speed into the lead in the *Wacky Races*, I 'accidentally' release an oil slick behind me. Good so far. But, instead of closing, the release flap catches on a rock, spinning the car around and sending it back into the oil slick. As the *Mean Machine* twirls like a ballerina, my competitors speed past, dodging the slick. Do I mope and weep like a baby? No, reader. I wait until the car stops spinning, then I tie Muttley to a broom handle and use him to mop up the slick so that I can drive on to complete the race. Up and back at 'em, see? Still, I come last.

I launch Klunk's feather-seeking missile to catch that pigeon. That beaky-bozo ducks (*snigger*) as the missile whizzes by, pulling off a feather in its wake. Said feather floats gently down to alight on the nose of the unsuspecting Dastardly, just as the missile realigns itself to the nearest feather. The one on my nose. BAM! Do I throw in my medals? No, I take a blasting from the Gen-er-al and get back into the *Flying Machine* like a soldier. 'Te-en-shun!' We still haven't caught that foul flying rat.

My next despicable plan is to explode the world's largest balloon when the Racers drive by, blowing them to kingdom come. Muttley is armed with a pea-shooter to burst the rubber bubble. However, as I'm blowing up the balloon, it starts to float upwards, taking me with it. On my command, "Muttley, get me down, immediately!", Muttley pops the balloon with the pea-shooter, and I plummet to earth. Do I throw myself over a precipice? No, no, no! I merely emit a long, "Curses, drat and phooey!" then I'm back in the race. See, one of life's unstoppables, that's me.

So reader, what can we learn from all this? There's a lesson here somewhere, as Spaaace Ghooost would say. And that lesson is this: 'if you slip on life's banana skin, get up, wipe off the stains and carry on'.

And remember, leave the skin on the ground for the next idiot.

Dastardly Words to Inspire . . .

"Don't just stand there sniggering – do something!"

"Look you, Muttley, make with the nasty laugh."

"Right, I'm going to win this race fair and square, even if I have to cheat to do it."

"We'll wait here until I think of something unspeakable."

"This scheme is so dastardly, it even scares me!"

"Don't just stand there, Muttley. Find a chisel and get me out!"

"Drat, I can't do any dirty work from back here, I'll cheat my way up front."

"Oh drat the luck, we're stuck in a mudhole."

"Hmm, I'm beginning to get an idea for a dirty trick."

"Ye gads, a real steer!"

50

60 SECOND INTERVIEW THE HOODED CLAW

Well hi . . . Colm N. Tater here. Welcome to the hot spot, to give us a little bolus of his life's philosophy in one minute or less, Sylvester Sneekley, aka The Hooded Claw!

SS: Blast! No one is supposed to know who I am. I'd really rather prefer it if you didn't print this. Just call me the Claw.

CT: Er, sure thing, Clawy. So, by day you're a self-respecting gentleman should she have it all? Why not just a little crumb for Clawy? Or a slice? Or the whole darn cake! With her out of the way, I'd inherit everything. And then the world would have to take notice. They'd have to SEE Sylvester Sneekley.

CT: OK, OK, so you're a nobody. The question on everyone's lips is this: you and your bumbling henchmen, the Bully Brothers, against one 'lil' ol' damsel' and you still haven't done her in! Why not?

HC: Pah! If you only knew what she's capable of! All

CHAPTER 3

LIFESTYLE AND

LIVELIHOOD

TOP CAT'S GUIDE TO

Mischievous. Fanciful. Crafty. Call him what you will, Top Cat is a streetwise hukster who never tires of get-rich-quick schemes, scams and fanciful impersonations. Nurture your own street-smart mindset with TC's tips for staying on top in a dog-eat-dog world.

Take Control

• You gotta to be the indisputable leader o' the gang. Be the boss. Be the VIP. Be the championship. Be the most tip-top, top cat!

• If your gang discovers a picnic basket containing a baby, it's up to you to pilfer milk bottles and keep the child fed. Ya know what I mean?

• Be spectacular with your vernacular – if you want to be the chief, you gotta talk like the chief.

Operate with Integrity

• A cat with principles is a cat with integrity. So, if TC happens to come across a suitcase packed full o' money, the fine principle of 'finders-keepers' means ... TC is rich!

• Do something to help an ol' lady: she might remember you in her will.

• If you meet a billionaire philanthropist, act needy – integrity ain't everything.

Play it Cool

• Whether you happen to be posing as a millionaire oil sheikh or feigning a down-and-out tale to win some money, always stay cool, in control and perfectly confident of your own abilities.

• If you discover that your best-laid plans have holes in them, or flattery gets you nowhere, you better be able come up with a new plan in a dash.

Cultivate the Clan

• Remember, a superficial crush on the poetry-loving she-line next door is no match for real friendship.

• Surround yourself with a motley crew of fine feline fellas. Take my clan: Fancy-Fancy is my right-hand man; Benny the Ball may be slow, but he's not stupid;

Fancy-Fancy

Spook

STAYING ON TOP

Choo-Choo is enthusiastic and devoted; Brain looks after the money — it's the purr-fect set up.

• Make sure that your pals are more naïve than yo' ... after all, you don't want them toppling the chief. That would be a cat-astrophe!

Acquire the Look

• Never underestimate the importance of fashion. Look at me. You could say that I am the definition of 'dernier cri' ... 'en vogue', so to speak. A purple vest and a natty straw hat is a configuration fit for a chief with a laid-back disposition, such as yours truly.

• If you're short, you'd better be savvy — just ask Benny the Ball. (Now that's funny, very funny!)

Take a Risk

• Feign a disease to meet a beautiful nurse — then let your considerable charm do the rest. (If the nurse turns out to be mangy, you can always make a miraculous recovery.)

• Like, you get a knock on the head, and yo' pals think that your life's in danger? Take advantage of it. Who knows what they'll be prepared to do for you?

• If one of your pals meets the description of a missing heir ... do I really need to go on?

Benny the Ball · Choo-Choo · Brain

Dos and Don'ts for Top Cats

1. **Do** be resourceful.
2. **Don't** get caught without a plan.
3. **Do** be ready for action.
4. **Don't** lose your cool.
5. **Do** be loyal.
6. **Don't** disturb your leader's slumber for a crossword puzzle.
7. **Do** dress for success.
8. **Don't** dress like Officer Dibble (Dribble).
9. **Do** live, live, live!
10. **Don't** lose your enthusiasm.
11. **Do** get rich.
12. **Don't** get caught.

Top Tips for Relaxing

A selection of the mellowest moves from our
scintillating line-up of cartoon cronies.
Here's how our 2-D darlings get their kicks.

Wilma

Pop a batch of apatosaurus patties into the fire-pit or whip up a pile of pteranodon-egg-white meringues. I find baking so soothing for the nerves; also, Fred's too 'caveman' to step into the kitchen so I get a bit of peace.

Fred

You can't beat floating around in your own backyard swimming pool. Ha, ha, Barney and me built one between our pads. I spend the few moments I have to myself bobbing around, cactus home-brew in one hand, megalith sandwich in the other. Ahh!

Dick Dastardly

Relax? I don't have time to relax! I've schemes to scheme, plots to plot and plans to plan. When I sit down, my mind boils with evil ideas and strategies so unspeakably foul that even I baulk at them (a little). I guess that is how I relax.

Hong Kong Phooey

Ah'm a regular kinda guy, ah jus' takes in a ball game or throws some shapes, like a Hong Kong Phooey chop — Ha!

Captain Caveman

Huh. Relax. Mmmm. Me just look at Dee Dee. Unga zowie! All of me go floppy. Hmm.

George Jetson

I guess I'm an old-fashioned kinda guy at heart. I love to kick back in my favourite armchair while Rosie the Robot brings my slippers, a drink and wires me up to the Mood Mellower™ to play something soothing into my auditory cortex.

Yogi Bear

There's nothing like takin' a stroll in the woods to chill a bear out and give him an appetite. Which way to the Flintstones'? I could wrap myself around that old megalith sandwich and not leave a crumb.

Top Cat

I'm the King o' Cool. TC is always relaxed. Even when I'm asleep.

60 SECOND INTERVIEW DICK DASTARDLY

Hey, hey, hey folks, it's Colm N. Tater here with Mr Sunshine himself, Dick Dastardly. Dick, you've got 60 seconds to spread a little joie de vivre. Ready? Go!

DD: "Schwa duh" what? Don't waste my time, man. What are you talking about? Are you lot back again? What now?

CT: Well, we just wanted to learn a little more about the man. What makes Dick Dastardly tick?

DD: Foul deeds, man. Using any means necessary – or unnecessary – to get my own way and that way's the winning way. *(Chortle.)*

CT: Anyone reading this is likely to be a lost soul in need of some comfort and advice. Does the great Dick Dastardly have any to offer?

DD: Plenty. Listen up, fools. There's only one winner. What does that make the others? Second, third, fourth? No, sirree.

Losers. L-O-O-s ... er well, you get the picture. I use every ounce of wit to get myself to the front and stay there. Fair play is for fools and fair-players. Ridiculous. Dream some dreams, men, scheme some schemes ... don't let your conscience hold you back. I never have and look where it's gotten me? ... Drat.

CT: You have a fairly unforgiving attitude. What happened in your life to make you so cynical?

DD: Pah! Not a cynic? Then you're a cissy! If you must know, the school of hard knocks taught me all I know. And that is, if you don't have it, connive until you do. I was a lonely child. No one would play with me because I stole their toys and pretended they were mine. Then the misadventure with Dolores and her Dancing Dogs (don't you raise a querulous eyebrow, clunk-head. Get my agent on the line.). Life has taught me that the winner takes it all. The loser has to fall.
(Trots off, humming a tune that was not to feature in the Pit Parade for another decade or more.)

CT: Well, that's all folks. Learn at the knee of the master. Ahem.

Top Gadgets
with George Jetson

Why have a piece about gadgets in a lifestyle book, I hear you cry? Because they are designed to make your life easier and less stressful. Come with me, George Jetson, on an adventure into knobs and dials, and I'll show you how to streamline your life.

Jet Cars

Pros: when I think how my grandparents used to travel in an automobile, on highways, I have to laugh. Crazy. It must have taken forever and a day to get to Rio or England, London. The jetcar simply glides along using anti-gravity in the altitude stream you choose. Accidents are avoided by built-in anti-magnetic forcefields. It's simple.

Cons: the compact version, which I use for work, folds into a suitcase, but it's pretty darn tiny inside and you come out hunchbacked 'cos the dome's too low. The latest models have plasma-domes. Maybe one day . . .

Domestic Robots

Pros: like the perfect wife and mother rolled into one, these little beauties greet you with your slippers, present you with your drink, clean, tidy, iron, cook, put the dog on the treadmill, everything. Just get one.

Cons: if you buy a cheap, second-hand one, they can start to get a bit neurotic. There's nothing as annoying as a self-pitying robot.

3-D TVs

Pros: it makes me all nostalgic to think of the HDTV we had when I was a kid. Now you can get up and walk around your programme, if you can be bothered.

Cons: they still haven't solved the lost remote control issue.

Video Phones and Smart-Me Accessories

Pros: of course, video phones have been around since the Dawn of Man and work pretty well. It's the accessories that make it what it is today. Read on . . .

Cons: privacy has always been an issue. You can't tell your boss you've got moonpox if he can see your face. Or what if someone super-attractive calls after you've just got out of bed? That's where the Smart-Me™ comes in. Just hover it over your own ugly mug, and a washed and brushed version of you appears. Jane loves it because it plasters on even more make-up than usual, and the Crystal Glaze™ gives her a serene glow. She reckons . . .

Teleporters

Pros: these are so great! They cost a bomb, but you can get yourself anywhere in no time at all. Don't tell Jane, but I was running late on our wedding day

so I traded in the auto-vac and spent the proceeds on a trip down the aisle. I'm not sure she believed the auto-vac hoovered itself up. Some things never change.

Cons: it can get a bit messy. There has been the odd freak accident with flies and all, but it's never happened

to anyone I know. Apart from Al. His pet hamster was hibernating in his coat pocket. Poor Al.

Auto Walkways

Pros: glide to the shops or around the home on an auto walkway without moving a muscle.

Cons: the lack of movement puts a guy in a trance. Boy, oh boy, is it annoying when you find you've been around the room three times and still haven't got what you set out for.

Auto-Food-Delivery Systems

Pros: you want bacon and eggs-over-easy, you press a button and the food appears, piping hot, with sides, ready to eat. There's no preparation, no cooking, no arguing, no kooky recipes that the wife wants to 'try out' on the guinea pig (you!).

Cons: it's early days for this machine, and it's not glitch-free. You do sometimes get a roast egg or coffee sweetened with ketchup, but when it works, gee-whizz!

So, reader, stop mooching in the middle ages and get yourself some proper gear to make life a little smoother round the edges. Or have your robot get it for you.

What's in My Basket?
by Yogi Bear

Hey, hey, hey, folks, it's your ol' pal Yogi, giving you the lowdown on life the way I sees it — and I might let you sneak a peek in my pic-a-nic basket too.

The way I sees it, the hamper of life is full to bustin' and it's up to you to take as much as you can.

Lonely?
There's blueberry pie to share (you gotta be pretty lonely!)

Angry?
Cool off with a long slurp of lemonade.

Bored?
Eat that pickled chilli and life suddenly gets much more exciting.

Broke?
Nick the pic-a-nic from those that have. You're doing them a favour helping them stay slim.

Had a tiff with the one you're wiv?

Try a piece of peace-offering pie to bring them round to your way of thinking.

Stuck in a rut?

Swap your usual egg mayo for a Cajun chicken and jelly, you'd be amazed how different you feel. Just watch that tie!

Sick?

You know that they say about apples and doctors. A whole fruit bowl's gonna cure it all.

So get out into the great outdoors and go foraging for a spot of life-giving grub. Boy am I hungry. Boo Boo, let's go!

Working with Animals (and other Dumb Creatures)

by Dick Dastardly

Never work with animals. Or humans. That's my advice. Luckily, I'm the master of many skills, the Adonis of animals. No doubt, you'll have admired my way with these and other dumb creatures in *Wacky Races* and *Dastardly and Muttley in the Flying Machine*. Permit me to share with you, dear reader, a few pointers on pets, advice on animals and direction on dumb creatures.

Muttley

My glittering career has brought me into contact with many animals, not least the infamous Muttley. He has his uses, I grant you: as my sidekick and henchman, he provides an ugly, smelly counterpoint to my refined and sophisticated character.

Remarkably, his greatest trait, in fact, is his evil snigger. I have only to issue the command, "Look you, Muttley, make with the nasty laugh," and the imbecile chuckles in an arrestingly sinister fashion. Inexplicably, it seems to have become something of a catchphrase among the lesser-brained of this world.

If you are a close observer of my career, you will not have failed to notice that a significant amount of my disasters occur due to Muttley's stupidity. There was the unfortunate incident where I got covered in quick-drying cement and 'disaster-dog' decided to blast me out with dynamite. Or when Muttley had control of the pea-shooter when I was abducted by a giant balloon and I asked him to get me down . . . Need I go on?

Yet, of course, a man's best friend is his dog . . . When Muttley rolls over for a tickly-tum, fool that I am, I can't help but oblige, not least because he won't do a thing I ask 'til he gets his treat. Pathetic.

Yankee Doodle Pigeon

The very thought of that verminous birdie is enough to

get my ticker pounding! That flying fool! That drumstick on wings! Why, if I catch that mailbagged moron, I'll use him as a duster! To think I waste my energies – and risk my aristocratic neck – trying to catch that creature week after week. I can hardly bear to think about it. Ye gads!

Bum Steer

Of course, in the line of duty, I've come across a whole darn cattleyard of bulls and burros, each more vicious than the last. What about the amorous steer that approached my inflatable 'cow-on-the-highway' booby-trap and took exception when I tried to get in his way? Or the donkey that I accidently bought for 100 pesos (strictly in the line of duty, you'll understand) but when I tried to remove him from my car, kicked the *Mean Machine* to smithereens!

Klunk and Zilli

Of course, animals are not the only dumb creatures that one is forced to work with in the name of national

security. Klunk and Zilli really are as stupid as they look. One's so afraid of his own shadow that he only goes out after dark; the other makes crackpot inventions that never work and only speaks in beeps and whistles. Talk about low-budget. Really.

Well friends, I hope you have heeded my advice never to work with animals, unless you are a banker, of course. Until next time, Dastardly fans.

SECRET SQUIRREL'S
GUIDE TO
SELF-ARMING

Now, lookey here, guys and gals. If those kooks are making the hairs on the back of your neck stand up (see pages 44–46), it's time to equip yourself with some top gadgets and put yourself back in the driving seat. Just blast away that stress. Here are my favourite contraptions.

HAMMER COIN

When you flick the coin on to the table, a hammer on an extendable arm pops out and cracks your opponent on the noggin. Handy too if you find a raised nail is snagging your cashmere . . .

LASER HAT

At the press of a button, your lid lifts and a laser gun takes out your enemy in one quick fizzle. A stylish solution to eliminate unwanted companions at weddings. As easy as One-Two-Smash!

"You gotta keep tricks up your sleeve . . . a bullet proof coat, a cannon hat, a machine gun cane with a RAT, TAT, TAT, RAT!"

THE FLAME-THROWER

An oldie, but goodie, this little beauty can charcoal your nemesis or cremate your steak in a flash. Handle with caution — you don't want to singe your bushy tail, eh?

FREEZE-RAY

Use this cool contraption to encase your enemy in a block of ice or chill a dame's martini to perfection, your call.

THE ATOMISER

A gadget of joy for the technophile, this innocent-looking grey box turns you atom-sized in a flash. So, it's into the ear of your rival and start causing mayhem. It's wise to have someone ready to turn the dial that makes you large again, since as a micron, shifting that dial is the equivalent of lifting the Statue of Liberty with your little finger. Tricky. Pretty tricky.

BUG RING

And if you love all things miniature, try the Bug Ring! Flip the gemstone and a tiny flying carnivore jumps out and sinks its jaws into any nose that's stuck in your business. Not advisable for use as a love token (unless you're trying to end it).

There are so many gadgets available without a licence on the black market, you just gotta know who to ask. Try the 'Super-Giggle Gas Bomb' or 'Wristwatch Vice' for discreet protection, or fit a 'Frying Pan Button' to your jacket. More drastically, a 'Heat-ray Glass Eye' goes with you wherever you are.

REMEMBER AGENTS,
PROTECTION IS POWER.

TOP CAT'S
DRESSING
FOR
SUCCESS

So, yowse back for more, eh? Can't say I blame ya, reader, can't say I blame ya at all. Your very own Top Cat ain't no chump when it comes to dressing like a champ.

So, like, er, Benny says to me, "Gee, TC, how'd you stay so slick?" And I says, "Elemental, my dear Benny. El-e-MEN-tal."

1 Starting at the top, where every cat should be: get yourself a super-smart boater. No need to bother your tailor, just cast a fishing rod over the old school gates and hook yourself a hat when those kiddies run by. Check that shade, there, my friend, check that shade. If it ain't in a colour to your liking, throw that fishy back and try another school.

2 Next, whiskers. You may think I sport this fine foliage to maintain my feline integrity. You may be right. But take a look at this fine visage here, do they not add a certain something, I asks you? A little bit of class to the act? Nothing appears by accident, it's all design, pal, all design.

3 So, you're eyeing up the waistcoat, eh? Now, wait a minute there, let-a me guess, you're thinking, "I can't get a fit like that! That cool cat's got one A-class tailor." But — and let's keep this hush-hush-hush, eh boys? — I found it in a trash can! That day, the cat gods were smiling (and Dibble was at the dogs). A little rummaging brought forth untold rewards — well, some fish bones and this fine garment. Not bad for a day's labour, eh?

So whaddaya waitin' for? Get out there and get yourself some glad rags in the TC style. Not EX-actly the same, of course, you don't wanna trash the look of the King o' the Alley. But you can sniff my coat-tails if you catch my drift . . . I say Me-OW!

Penelope Pitstop's Guide to Using Your Talents

We-ell, howdy, sugahs. Just a lil' ol' gal from the South, bringing you some top tips on usin' what you got and loving yo-sel'. Ah'm just a damsel tryin' to find mah way through life, but Ah know what momma told me: "Hon, ain't nobody gonna love you, unless you love yo-sel'." And that's what ah'm gonna teach you.

Looks

Every gal knows you gotta make the most of yo' looks. Ah favour a traditional beauty routine of good old-fashioned soap 'n' water, followed by face cream, foundation, rouge, eyeliner, mascara, lipliner, lipstick, oh, and powder – lots! Then for the hair, brush one hundred times to bring up a shine, then back comb into a ponytail, add loads of lacquer and you're all finished. There now, that wasn't so hard, was it?

Talent

You gotta make the most of what you got. Ah like to capitalise upon my assets every day. Take driving, for instance. Ah am a good driver, if you'll allow for my immodesty. Ah do like to get behind the wheel and show those boys what ah can do. And then if ah have a lil' ol' problem, one of those gallant gents will come racing to rescue 'Pretty Penny' outta the goodness of their hearts. People are so sweet.

Charm

Where would we be without a little charm in the world? How nice it is when someone shows some manners. Silly ol' me once left my indicator on for the whole race while ah was fixing my makeup and those lil'ol' Wacky Racer boys all drove along behind me, waiting for me to make mah turn. Whoops! Ah gave them all a kiss on the podium to say sorry and only grumpy Dick Dastardly seemed to mind.

Believe in Yo-sel'

Ah don't mind being the only gal to whirl her wheels in Wacky Races: ah'm glad to show what gals can do with their talents. 'The Glamour Gal of the Gas Pedal', they call me. Ah can even complete top secret missions with that nasty ol' Hooded Claw nipping at my white leatherette heels, as long as ah have those rollicking rescuers, the Ant Hill Mob, to protect me. Ah believe, ah achieve. That's my motto. Along with "Hey-ulp, hey-ulp!" But what's a gal to do?

Toodle-loo, y'all. x

Top Cat's Guide to Staying

So, you're back down the alley, rat-tat-tatting on ol' TC's tin roof and asking, "TC, how do I stay as cool as you when life gets sticky?" Well, pal, it's like this . . .

Stress at Work

What's the stress? What's the trauma? You need to relax. Take it easy. Like I says, "I'll find work tomorrow, Ma." The only stress in my life is from Officer Dibble. He's always loitering with intent — to spoil my fun. I say to him, "Officer, you look tired. The city's number-one policeman needs to take it easy. Here's you are. Officer, relax, chill out, take ten on this old sofa here. TC and the boys will step down to the store, quick sharp, hup-two, hup-two, and pick you up a coffee and a donut. Just slip us ten bucks, Officer, and we'll be on our way." I take control, confront the stress and look for a way to turn it to my advantage.

Slick Under Stress

Domestic Strife

I lead the life of a bachelor prince. I have the perfect apartment, bijou but well appointed with magnificent views of my kingdom, the alley. I have availed myself of all the mod-cons, including mood lighting (or eyemask); soundproofing (you may know them as earplugs); and my own telephone . . . well, the good officer's police phone. I say to the boys, "Fellas, fellas, make the most of what you've got and if it isn't good enough, borrow someone else's."

Financial Worries

Where's the drama? The street is my store: I find everything I need right on my doorstep. I take care who I 'touch', it's a crazy cat who fouls his own patch, 'scuse the expression. We take what we need when our very own boy in blue doesn't interfere. But, of course, the boys are also keen to keep Dibble company on his lunchbreak, and even when Dib tried switching cabs, he couldn't give Choo-Choo the slip. So we pop in on our favourite cop and

When it comes to she-lines, I leave that to Fancy . . . he's got all the moves and can charm a puss out of her boots. I try not to get involved. Of course, all the gals like the leader of the pack, but this is one Top Cat that ain't gonna get pounced on.

feign 'death by starvation of the King of the Alley' 'til we get our special with sides. Dibble pays up and the boys join me for a slap-up feed. How's that for slick? If you need it, ask, if you don't get it, take it.

So, when life gets to smell a little pungent, close the lid of your trash can and take a cap nap. That's the way, fellas, that's the way.

Polishing your Image with

Pip, pip! Peter's the name, perfection's the game. Let me tell you a thing or two about polishing up your act. Believe me buddy, you need to. Life may have dragged you down a bit, but there's no reason just to let it all go. No! Never fear, I'm your man.

Dress Up to the Mark

A smooth style tells the world that your feathers can't be ruffled. It inspires confidence, says "I'm a leader", lets 'em know who's boss. So get to the barber's for a short back and sides, then get the ironing board out and press your glad rags to kingdom come.

Arrive in Style

Believe me, pal, it's all part of the bigger picture. Shoot up the drive in a freshly polished, racing red roadster, spraying gravel as you spin to a standstill and you'll have 'em eating out of your knitted driving gloves. Environmental concerns are all very well for girls and hippies, let them worry about it. You've got something to show, and it's big and red.

Talk the Talk

Now here's where you play it clever. Damsels like the softly-softly approach so instead of 'bestride(-ing) the narrow world like a colossus' (or somebody), walk in with quiet confidence, take the hand of the eldest dame and plant

Peter Perfect

a smacker on it (yes, I know it's not Penelope Pitstop but just think of the rewards you'll reap). The gals will literally swoon. Now ask about them, talk tennis and flowers . . . and whatnot. Before long those little ladies will want to know more about their irresistible interlocutor and SNAP!, you got 'em. Now you can lay it on thick with a large helping of Peter Perfect Pie (as Mama used to say . . .).

L.T.W.

Leave Them Wanting. So you've indicated that there may be a Manhattan apartment, that the Jag's a pussycat if you know how to stroke her nicely, and that Mama and Father own half of England, London. But leave it there. Time to go. The honeybees always return to the hive.

I've said enough. Ciao.

60 SECOND INTERVIEW OFFICER DIBBLE

Stop in the name of the Law! Ha ha. I always wanted to use that line. Yes, sir, it's your old pal, Colm N. Tater, here. With me is our very own boy in blue, Officer Charlie Dibble. Let's find out how that cop copes.

CT: So, Officer, how'd you handle life with that filibustering feline, Top Cat, always causing you grief?

CD: Gee, eh, it's an honour to be here. Well, I have to keep 'em in check 'cos that TC gets one over on me at every opportunity. But, you know, I always say to him, "Knowing you guys is like being married. You can't live with 'em, and you can't live without 'em."

CT: Can't you just round them up and take them to the cat pound?

CD: TC and the gang drive me crazy but, truth is, life on the beat would be awful dull without Top Cat's hair-brained schemes to bust open. And he looks after me too. Like when I was in line for the Iron Man award for 3,000 days continuous service, with only one day to go to beat the record; but it was one of 'em days, banana skins on the pavement, open manholes, bank robberies, and me coming down with a helluva cold. Who was it kept me on the beat? TC and the gang.

CT: Why'd he wanna do that?

CD: Beat if I know. I guess he really likes me and wanted me to get that two-week vacation on full pay. Of course, with me outta the way he might think he could get back to his illegal activities unhampered. Little did he know that Sarge had laid on a troupe of three officers to pound my patch in my absence. I suppose that explains why TC and the gang turned up in my car en route to my fishing trip . . .

CT: So, er, Charlie, what does a cop do to relax after a long day pounding the pavements?

CD: Well. I like to throw on my zoot suit and head down the Hep Cat club to catch some jazz. Oh, and I do a little Cha Cha Cha class to keep fit. But mainly I just hang out in the alley with TC and the boys.

CT: What? You spend all day pursuing them and all evening chilling with them?

CD: Sure. We shoot the breeze, play a little cards, go fishing for dimes in the drains with a magnet . . . you know, mano-a-cato stuff.

CT: So I guess you're a TC fan?

CD: You could say that. We've all got our roles in life. Top Cat's is to get something for nothing, mine is to make him put it back.

CT: Thank you, Officer Dibble, for that interesting insight into life on the beat and off it.

CD: Sure, all in a day's work.

"I think better when I'm moving."

Top Cat

· A Little Moment of Calm ·

CHAPTER 5

SELF HELP

182226283133353739414345474951535557596163656769717375777981838587899193959799

CHARACTER QUIZ

We all have our aspirations, and what better to aspire to than a cartoon character? They live our dreams, they slip on our banana skins, but they don't feel our pain. What's not to like? Try out this quiz to see if you are a Fred, Dick, Barney or even a Top Cat himself. But first, decide which you aspire to be and see if you make the grade.

Q. Your best pal turns up for a night out in the most revolting shirt you've ever seen. Do you:

A. let him have the benefit of your honest opinion;

B. offer him your best shirt;

C. tell him what you think then make him wear one of your (least-favourite) shirts;

D. say nothing, his lack of cool makes you look better?

COLM N. TATER'S COLUMN
WHO ARE YOU?

Q. You find a delicious-looking sandwich, unattended. Do you:

A. eat it. Finders keepers;

B. ask who it belongs to;

C. pocket it, it may come in handy;

D. check what's in it before deciding on one of the above?

Q. You've been asked to step in as best man at short notice. Do you:

A. get up there and crack a few jokes. No one's expecting the Gettysburg Address;

B. beg your friend not to ask you. There must be someone else;

C. you're centre stage where you like to be, let 'em have it, both barrels;

D. ask how much the fee is?

Q. Your boss has spinach in her teeth. Do you:

A. tell her straight off;

B. gently suggest she may want to check a mirror;

C. make a joke of it;

D. don't point it out? Her problem.

CHARACTER QUIZ

COLM N. TATER'S COLUMN
WHO ARE YOU?

ANSWERS:

MOSTLY As:
You are **FRED FLINTSTONE**. Well, who's the bossy boots, then? You're a flamboyant extrovert who likes to tell it how it is but don't hold much truck with that listening stuff. If it's gotta happen, you da man or lady, but you don't like to look and learn.

MOSTLY Bs:
You are **BARNEY RUBBLE**. So, you're the amiable type and a bit of an introvert. OK, still waters run deep. Just take care that folks ain't fishing without a permit.

MOSTLY Cs:
You are **TOP CAT**. You've got the gift of the gab and you love to hold an audience. Expressing your opinion and holding centre stage ring-a-dings your bell.

MOSTLY Ds:
You are **DICK DASTARDLY**. You'll analyse a situation and make a plan but you have to know you're often misguided. Still, don't look down, eh?

THE SELF-HELP TRIANGLE

So folks, Colm N. Tater presented Dick Dastardly with a triangle of concepts necessary to engender self-belief, each word feeding the other, to see what he would make of it. Here are the results …

= ACCEPTANCE =

Ah, yes. I accept lots of things. I accept that my Dolores had her head turned by a phoney in a wig. I accept that I never, ever win, despite trying every dirty trick I can think of. I accept that the feathered fool continues to evade capture despite me undertaking flying manoeuvres worthy of the Red Baron. Yes, yes, I accept these things. Doesn't make them any better though does it? Move on, move on. What's next, dunderhead?

= LOVE =

Love? You talk to Richard M. Dastardly about love? With a past as tragic as mine and a future as bleak, where does dratted love come into it? The only time I feel a surge of passion is when looking at that devilishly handsome chap in the mirror, and I can't spend all day doing that, can I? What a load of piffle.

= TRUST =

Pah! The last time I trusted someone she danced the tongue-tango with that leonine Lothario. I trust myself, however, I know that one day my schemes and ploys will come good. On that day, I will be first over the finishing line, and the speed of my automobile will vacuum a certain feathered freak out of the sky and smash him to smithereens against my windscreen. What a golden moment that will be. And pigeon pie for tea. Ye gads, the sweet, sweet day!

The Joy of To-do Lists

with Wilma Flintstone

Well, hi there. When life gets hectic, I pull out a piece of slate and a chisel and just carve a little to-do list for myself. It's so therapeutic and clears the mind, leaving me free to worry about Fred's balding work pelt or where Dino's hidden the ammonite doorstop. Of course, it's no good sharing the list with Fred, he just says, "Oh gee, it's next on the list, Wilma!" and then sneaks out the back way and hides round at Barney's... 'til Betty sends him home again. Honestly, those boys!

Here's a typical list to show you what kind of things to note down. Oh, and, er, it's always a good idea to write a list for your spouse of those little jobs you don't fancy doing yourself!

See, my mind is so much clearer now. Try it! I'm off to make some horseshoe crab pâté. My Fred loves it in his sandwiches. Bye, for now!

Shopping
Iguanodon eggs
Bronto steaks
Granite-ola
Rock cakes (Fred thinks I make them. Bless.)
Sabre-tooth snackos
Pelt wash (Rose & Magnolia)
Pebble polish
Betty's birthday present – mudpack facial? New archaeoptryx hat feather? Stegosaurus tote?

Household chores
Clean the woolly mammoth shower – there's lichen growing on him.
Clear out the IceAge™ food safe – some of those ready meals are prehistoric!
Grind the boulder chair (Pebbles drew graffiti on it. How she got hold of a chisel, I'll never know.)

Fred's tasks
Tidy up the rock garden.
Clean out the pond – there's a dead plesiosaur in it.
Dig up the bones Dino buried in the lawn – it's like a mammoth's graveyard in there!
Re-carve the boulder-mobile's flat tyre.
Stop cleaning his golf clubs.
Stop sneaking off to Barney's.
Bring the cactus home-brew still down from the treehouse; I know it's there.

ANTHROPOMORPHIC ANIMALS
The Colm N. Tater Interviews

Ladies and gentlemen! Colm N. Tater here again. It's time to tickle those brain cells with a little look at the reasons why people like to watch cartoons and especially, those with animals doing human stuff. What's our problem, eh? Who better to ask than that wonder of the woods, the prince of the picnic, Yogi Bear and his little pal, Boo Boo.

CT: Yogi, why do you think man has a need to anthropomorphise animals and watch them on screen doing the things that we humans do?

YB: Now, I'm smarter than the av-er-age bear, but I dunno what you folks is goin' on about. Ant-fro-po-mor-fise animals? I got the animal bit. And it's got something to do with ants. Dey a nat-u-ral food source for the av-er-age bear, but I don't like the way the lil' tykes tickle on the way down. And you never know if you got 'em all or if one's doing a salsa on your eyebrow while you're trying to explain to a lay-dee friend all about afro-mo-poh-poh-ik animals. Now, where was I?

CT: We were talking about the reasons behind man's desire to make animals display human actions and reactions on screen? Do you think it's because we can identify our own actions, emotions and responses being played out in an uncomplicated and more importantly, non-emotionally demanding way?

BB: Gee, Yogi, that man's sayin' that you's like a human. It must be all the man-food you eat. And now I look at you, you're half-dressed in human clothes too. That collar and tie and your hat, they's like them grey-faced men that come in automobiles at weekends with all the kids and wives and—

YB: —And pic-a-nics! Let me at 'em, let me at 'em!

BB: But Yogi, you don't want to be like them.

YB: I do, I do, I do, Boo Boo! Dey get to eat all that super-dooper food from the baskets. What's the beef? Heh, heh, heh. Beef, geddit?

CT: Er, Yogi, do you think it's because people find it cathartic to watch our problems being experienced by someone else without feeling guilty because the cartoon isn't capable of suffering our emotional or physical pain? If you like, we can laugh, guilt-free, when they slip on our proverbial banana skins because they aren't human?

YB: Bananas! Yum! You keep the skin, pal, I'll have that yummy middle bit. Dis bear's droolin' at the very thought. Where's that banana you promised me? Huh? Huh?

BB: Der, Yogi, I fink he was askin' you about being a cartoon bear.

YB: A cart-what? I'm smarter than the av-er-age bear, but I got no clue what that bald monkey's on about. If he's got no food, let's make tracks, Boo Boo. We're sniffing at the wrong hamper. If you ask me, he's a few sandwiches short of a pic-a-nic himself. Let's shift, let's scrabble, let's scram!

Well folks, that was Yogi, resolving a philosophical question that has troubled man since pen met paper. All that remains to say, according to my script, is a quote from a guy named Francis Bacon (Bacon? Eh? Don't let that greedy bear hear!) who once said:

"Imagination was given to man to compensate him for what he is not; a sense of humour to console him for what he is."

Good point, well made.

The Yogic Sarnie

Hey, hey, hey, folks, it's Yogi Bear here to make sure this book leaves a nice taste in your mouth, so to speak. Listen, there ain't nothin' better at lifting your spirits than a lil' ol' sarnie. So next time yowse feelin' blue, wrap you'self round one-a deese bad boys.

Sit up straight, breathe deeply then begin chewing slowly. Eat, enjoy and see if things ain't jus-a-lil-bitty-bit better on the other side.

The 'Yogic Sarnie' Recipe:

1. Take two slices of bread.
   Spread butter thickly over each slice.

2. Open the fridge. Starting with the top shelf, remove each jar, take a glob of each and spread over the bread. You are aiming for at least five condiments, savoury or sweet.

3. Now, turn your attention to the jars in the fridge door. You are looking for pickles. Place at least three types of pickle on the condiment layer.

4. Back to fridge, shelf two and three. Find cheese, salami, ham. Place slices over the pickles to anchor them into the condiment layer.

5. Shelf four: seek cold leftovers. Take a lump, blob or slice. Weigh down the cheese-charcuterie layer with this.

6. Shelf five (big fridge): eggs. If you can find a hard-boiled one, job done, slice and place onto leftovers. If raw, cook in preferred style and place on to leftovers.

7. Salad drawer: this is optional but it does add colour. If required, place a frill of lettuce or tomato swirl on to the egg. Tip: use ketchup to draw on a tomato if you don't have one.

8. Now, place the second piece of bread on to the top the pile, and fix everything in place with a cocktail stick. If you have layered your sandwich correctly, you should not be able to cut it without squeezing the contents out. **DO NOT ATTEMPT TO CUT THE SANDWICH.**